Piano /Vocal / Guitar

· THE BEST OF · JEROME KERN

ISBN 0-7935-2790-2

This publication is not for sale in
the EC and/or Australia
or New Zealand.

HAL•LEONARD™
CORPORATION
7777 W. BLUEMOUND RD. P.O. BOX 13819 MILWAUKEE, WI 53213

INDEXED

ALL THE THINGS YOU ARE

from VERY WARM FOR MAY

Lyrics by OSCAR HAMMERSTEIN II
Music by JEROME KERN

Some day my hap-py arms will hold you, And some day I'll know that mo-ment di-vine, When all the things you are, are mine! mine!

BILL
from SHOW BOAT

Lyrics by P.G. WODEHOUSE and OSCAR HAMMERSTEIN II
Music by JEROME KERN

Andante moderato

I used to dream that I would dis-cov-er__ The per-fect lov-er some

He can't play golf, or ten-nis, or po-lo,__ Or sing a so-lo, or

day. I knew I'd re-cog-nize him If ev-er he

row. He is-n't half as hand-some As doz-ens of

CAN'T HELP LOVIN' DAT MAN
from SHOW BOAT

Lyrics by OSCAR HAMMERSTEIN II
Music by JEROME KERN

De an - gels done plan.

De chimb-ley's smok-in', De roof is leak-in' in, _____ But he don't

_seem to care, He can be hap-py Wid jus' a sip of

gin. _____ I ev - en loves him when

his kiss - es got gin._____

Refrain *(slowly)*

Fish got to swim and birds got to fly,___ I got to love___ one

man till I die,___ Can't help lov-in' dat man___ of

mine._____ Tell me he's la - zy,

tell me he's slow, Tell me I'm cra - zy, may - be, I know,—

Can't help lov - in' dat man— of mine._____

— When he goes a - way

Dat's a rain - y day, And when he comes

back dat day is fine,____ De sun will shine.

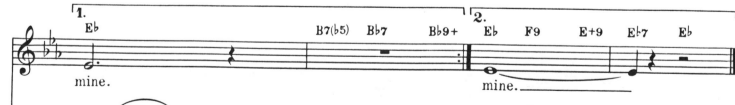

He can come home_ as late as can be,___ Home wid-out him_ ain't

no home to me,___ Can't help lov-in' dat man_ of

1. mine.

2. mine.____

CAN'T HELP SINGING

from CAN'T HELP SINGING

Words by E. Y. HARBURG
Music by JEROME KERN

Gracefully

Hum - ming bird, mock - ing bird, lis - ten to me; I got no

nest, I got no tree. Oh, but I'm hap - py as

Heav - en is wide; I got a song bub - bling in - side:

Refrain *(in bright waltz tempo)*

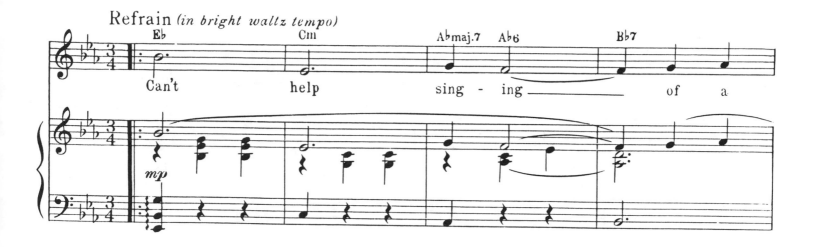

Can't help sing - ing _____ of a

prom - ise that A - pril is bring - ing, _____ I am

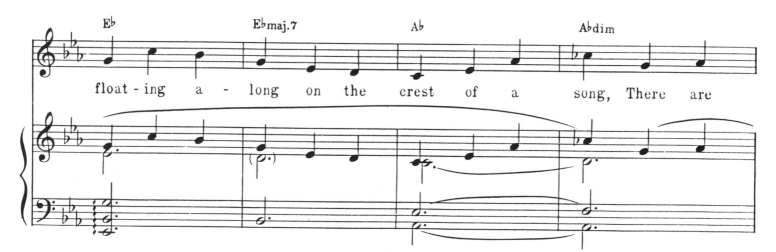

float - ing a - long on the crest of a song, There are

bells in my heart and they're ring - ing. _____

DON'T EVER LEAVE ME

from SWEET ADELINE

Lyrics by OSCAR HAMMERSTEIN II
Music by JEROME KERN

Refrain *(not fast)*

When you're a-way___ it's all wrong. I'm so de-pen-dent

When I need com-fort I al-ways run___ to you.

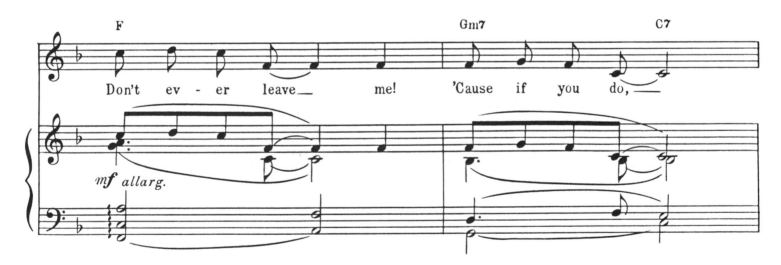

Don't ev-er leave___ me! 'Cause if you do,___

I'll have no one___ to run to.___ to.___

A FINE ROMANCE
from SWING TIME

Words by DOROTHY FIELDS
Music by JEROME KERN

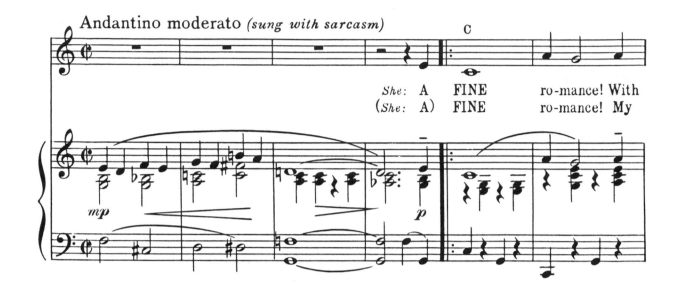

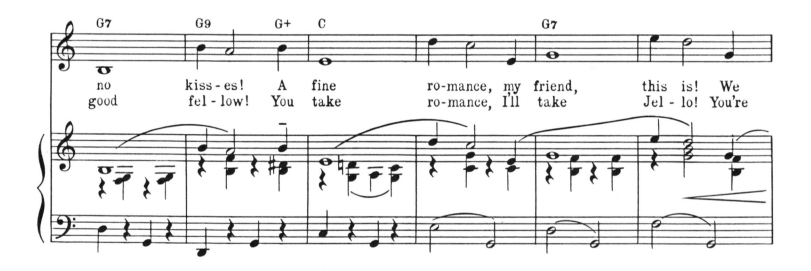

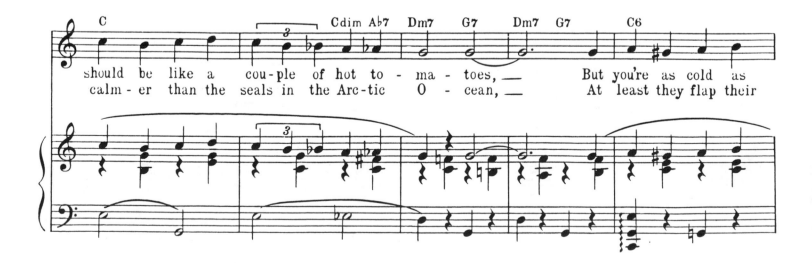

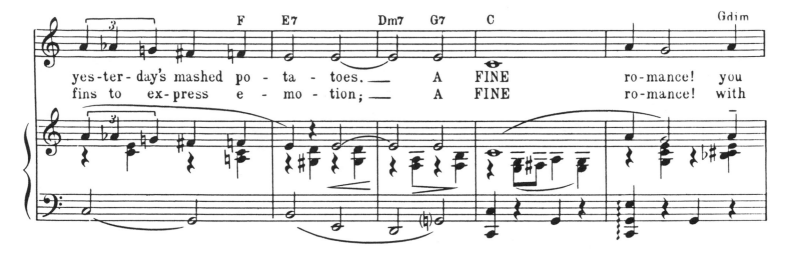

yes-ter-day's mashed po - ta - toes. ___ A FINE ro-mance! you
fins to ex-press e - mo - tion; ___ A FINE ro-mance! with

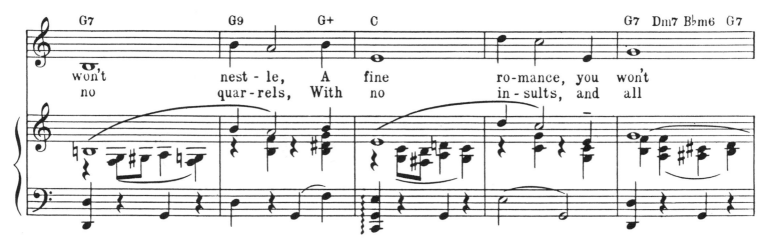

won't nest - le, A fine ro-mance, you won't
no quar-rels, With no in - sults, and all

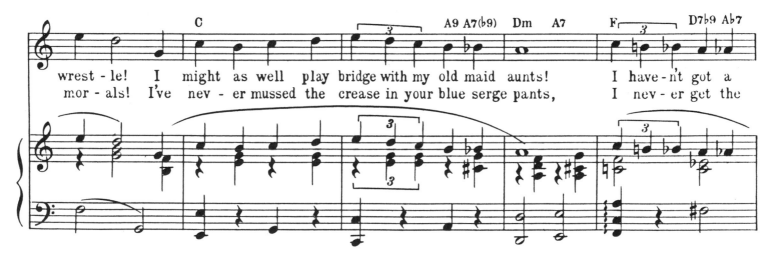

wrest - le! I might as well play bridge with my old maid aunts! I have-n't got a
mor - als! I've nev - er mussed the crease in your blue serge pants, I nev - er get the

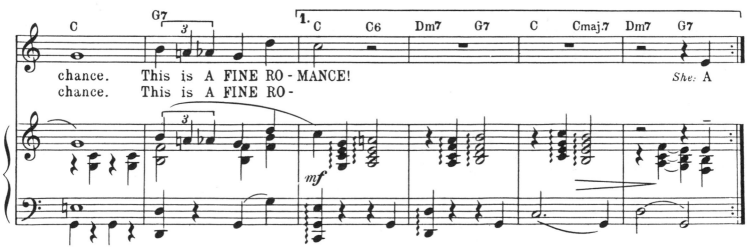

chance. This is A FINE RO - MANCE! *She:* A
chance. This is A FINE RO -

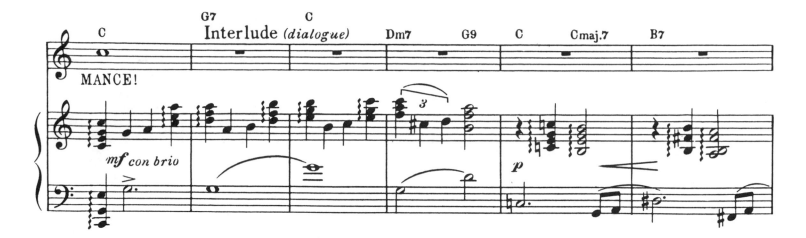

MANCE!

Interlude *(dialogue)*

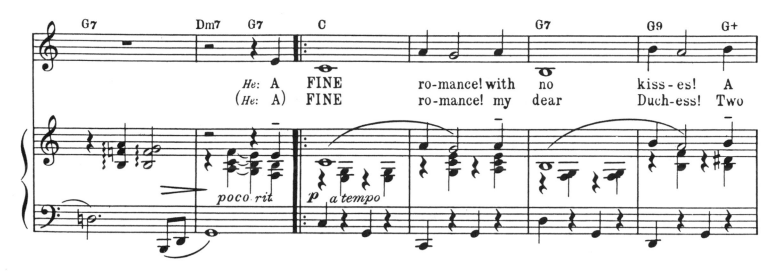

He: A FINE ro-mance! with no kiss-es! A
(He: A) FINE ro-mance! my dear Duch-ess! Two

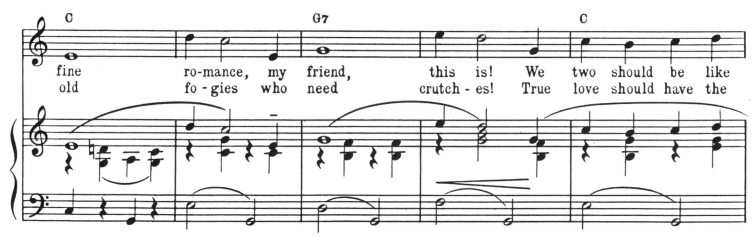

fine ro-mance, my friend, this is! We two should be like
old fo-gies who need crutch-es! True love should have the

clams in a dish of chow-der;___ But we just "fizz" like parts of a Seid-litz
thrills that a health-y crime has!___ We don't have half the thrill that the "March of

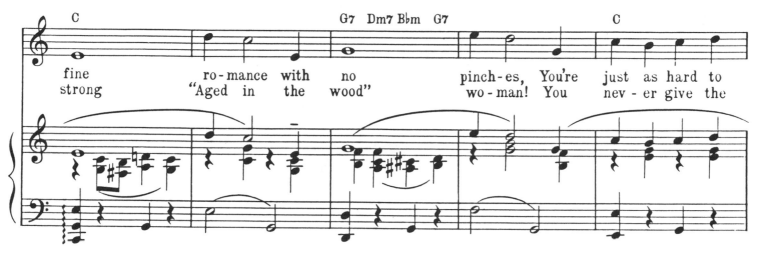

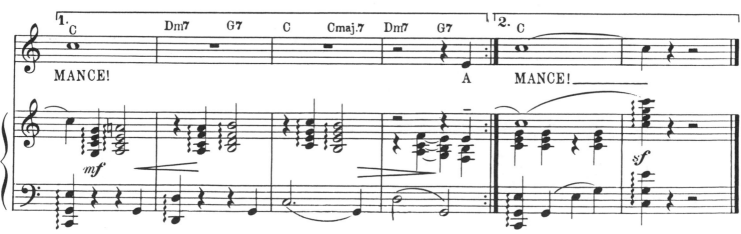

THE FOLKS WHO LIVE ON THE HILL

from HIGH, WIDE AND HANDSOME

Lyrics by OSCAR HAMMERSTEIN II
Music by JEROME KERN

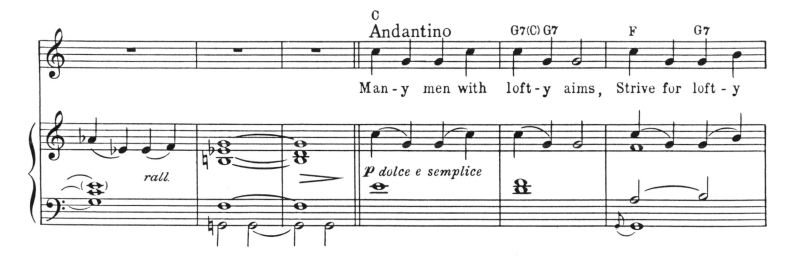

Man - y men with loft - y aims, Strive for loft - y

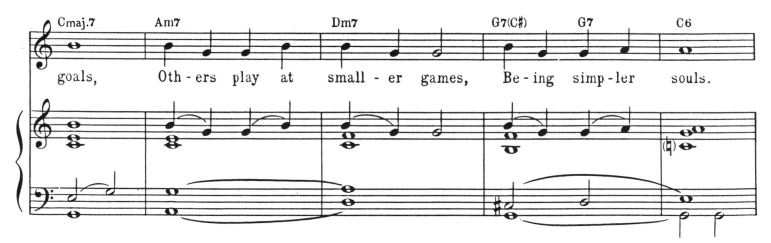

goals, Oth - ers play at small - er games, Be - ing simp - ler souls.

I am of the lat - ter brand; All I want to do Is to find a spot of land

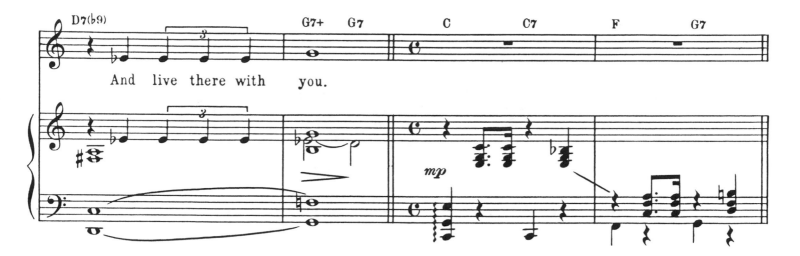

And live there with you.

Molto sostenuto

Some - day _____ we'll build a home on a hill top high,

You and I, ___ Shin - y and new_ a cot - tage that two_ can

fill. _____ And we'll be pleased to be called _____

"The folks who live on the hill!"

Some - day____ ____ we may be add - ing a thing or two,__

a wing or two___ We will make chang - es as an - y fam' - ly

will,_____ But we will al - ways be called____

"The folks who live on the hill."

Our ve-ran-da will com-mand a view of mead-ows green,— The sort of

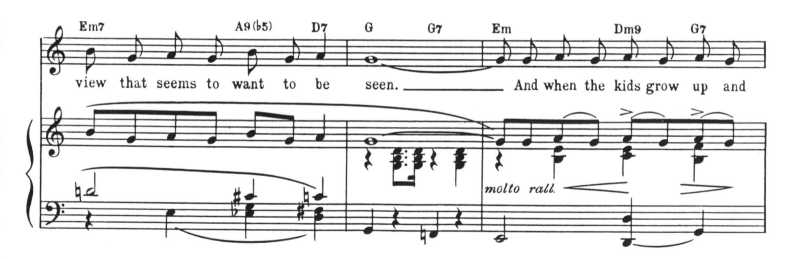

view that seems to want to be seen.———— And when the kids grow up and

leave us,——— We'll sit and look at that same old view,—

Just we two— Dar - by and Joan— who used to be Jack— and

Jill, _____ The folks who like to be called _____ What they have al-ways been called

"The folks who live on the hill."

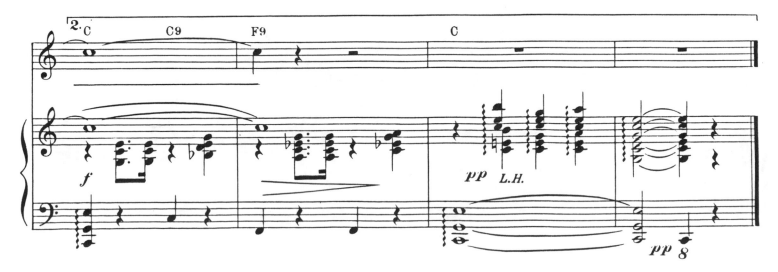

LONG AGO (AND FAR AWAY)
from COVER GIRL

Words by IRA GERSHWIN
Music by JEROME KERN

Drear - y days are o - ver. Life's a four - leaf clo - ver.

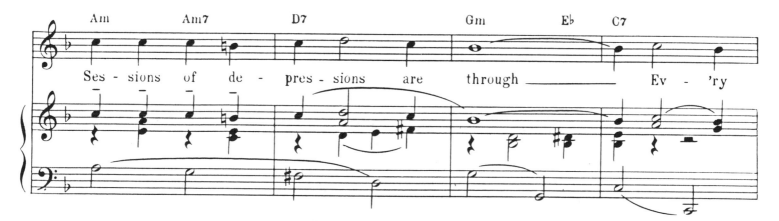

Ses - sions of de - pres - sions are through _____ Ev - 'ry

hope I longed for long a - go, comes true. _____

Refrain *(cantabile)*

Long a-go and far a-way, I dreamed a dream one

day And now that dream is here be-side me.

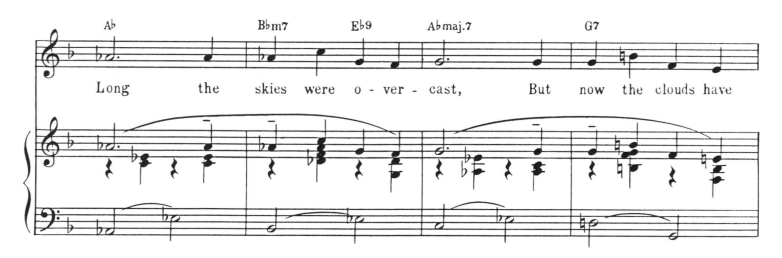

Long the skies were o-ver-cast, But now the clouds have

passed: You're here at last! _____ Chills run

up and down my spine, A - lad - din's lamp is mine, The dream I

dreamed was not de - nied me. Just one look and then I

knew _____ That all I longed for long a - go, was

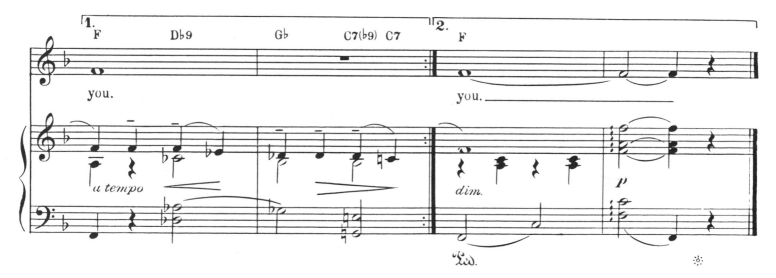

you.   you. _____

HOW'D YOU LIKE TO SPOON WITH ME

from THE EARL AND THE GIRL

Words by EDWARD LASKA
Music by JEROME KERN

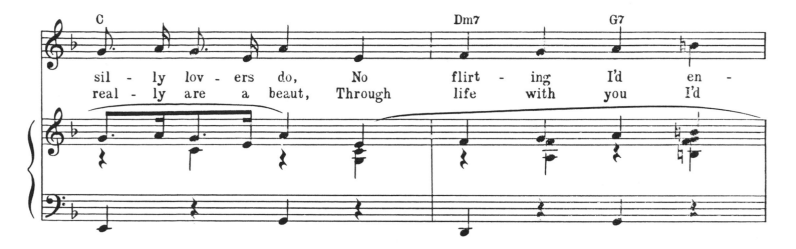

Refrain

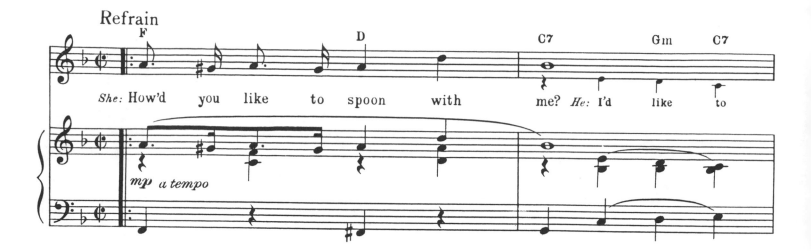

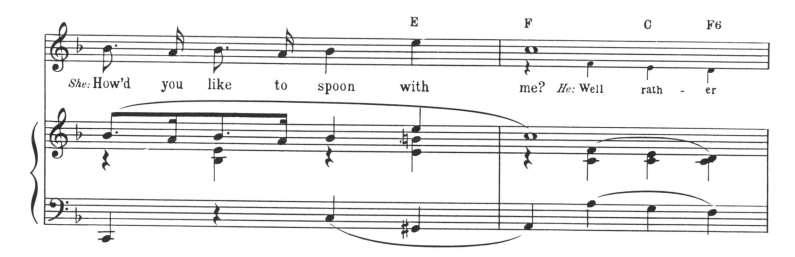

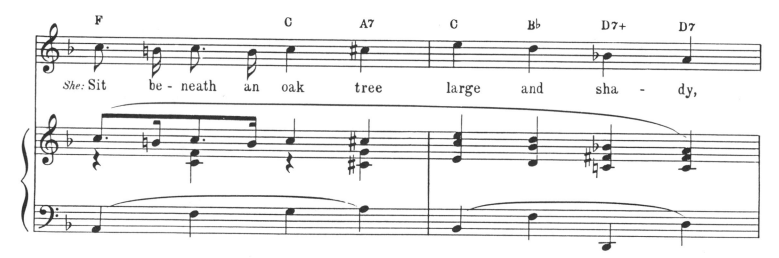

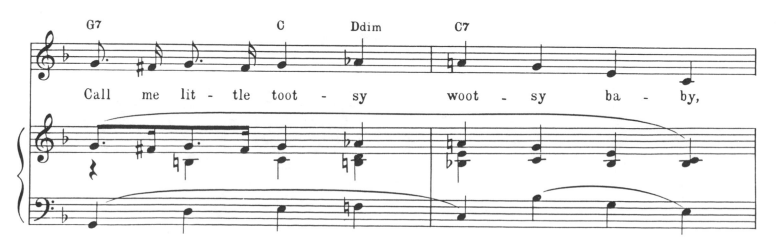

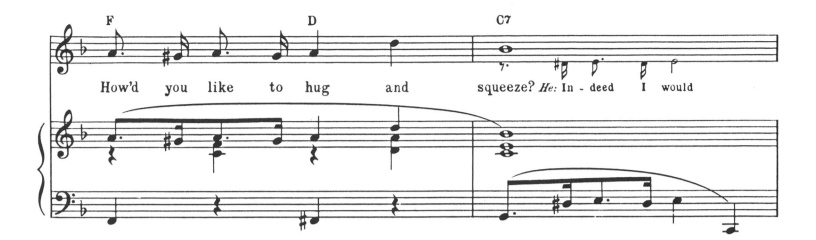

How'd you like to hug and squeeze? *He:* In - deed I would

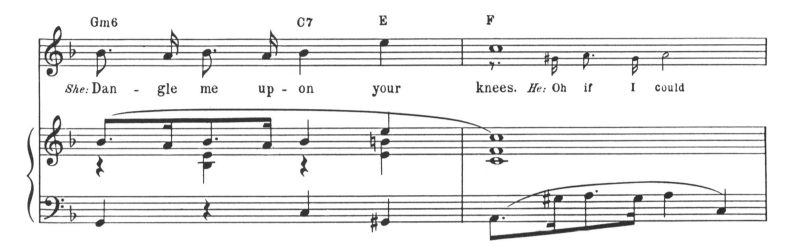

She: Dan - gle me up - on your knees. *He:* Oh if I could

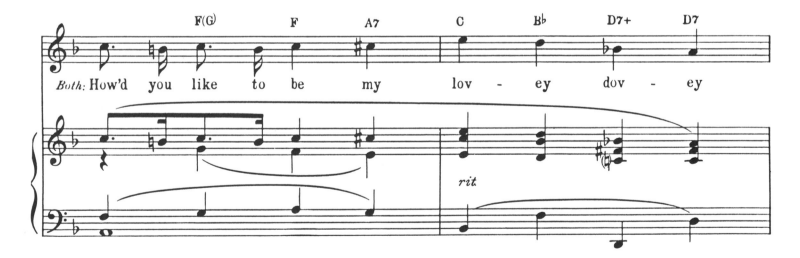

Both: How'd you like to be my lov - ey dov - ey

How'd you like to spoon with me? me?

I WON'T DANCE

from ROBERTA

Lyrics by OSCAR HAMMERSTEIN II and OTTO HARBACH
Screen Version by DOROTHY FIELDS and JIMMY McHUGH
Music by JEROME KERN

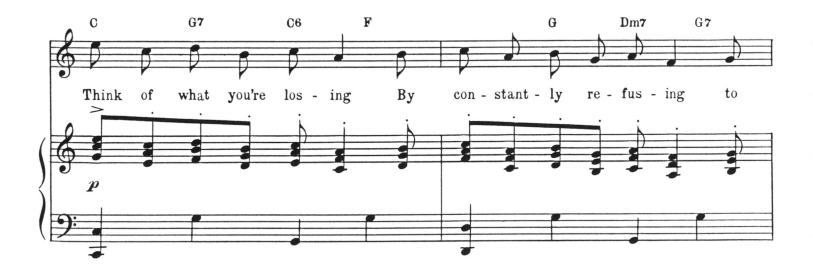

Think of what you're los-ing By con-stant-ly re-fus-ing to

dance with me._____ You'd be the i-dol of France with me!_____

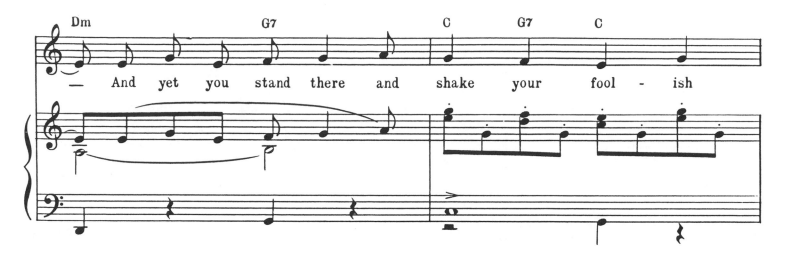

And yet you stand there and shake your fool - ish

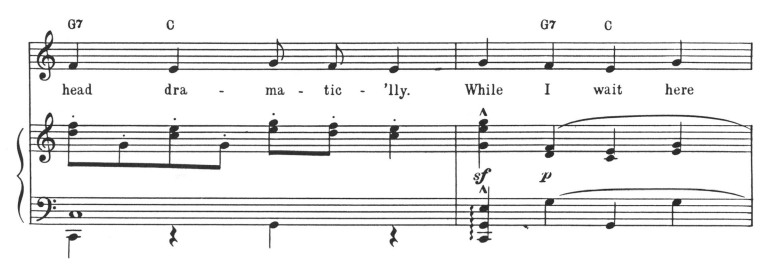

head dra - ma - tic - 'lly. While I wait here

So ec - sta - tic - 'lly You just look and say em - pha - tic - 'lly

L'istesso tempo

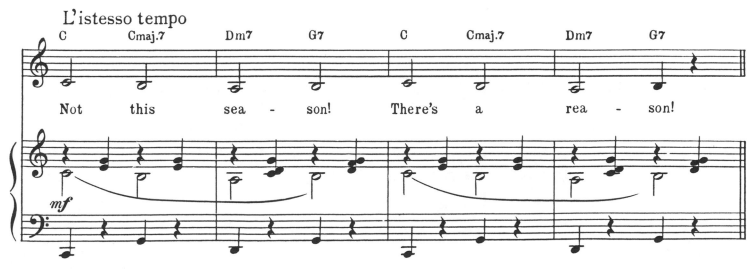

Not this sea - son! There's a rea - son!

38

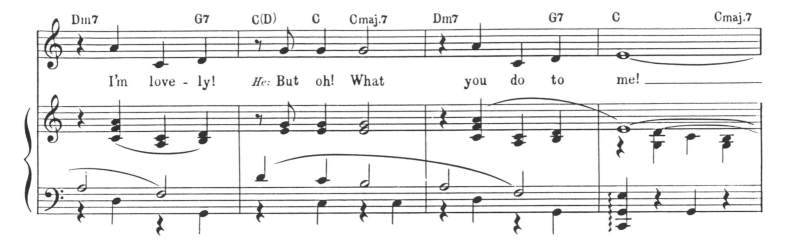

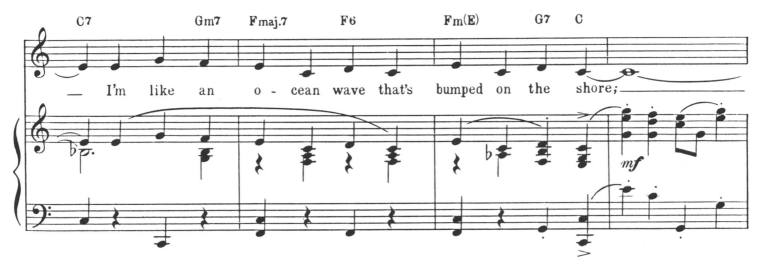

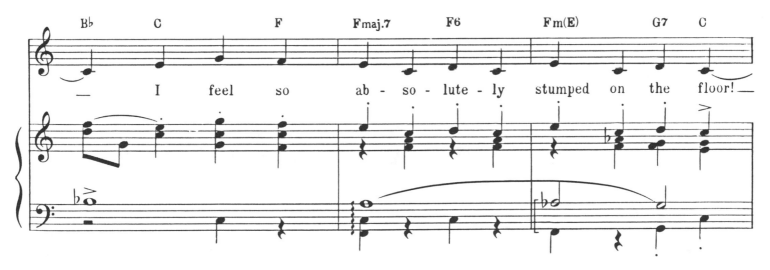

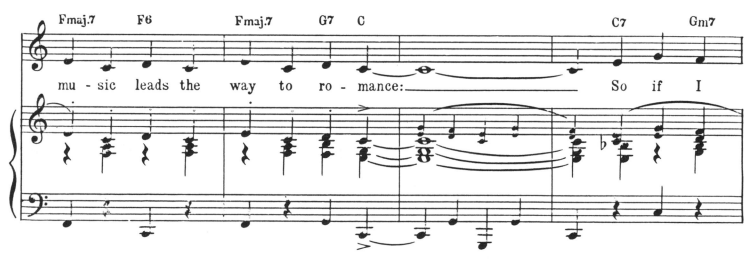

I'M OLD FASHIONED

from YOU WERE NEVER LOVELIER

Music by JEROME KERN
Words by JOHNNY MERCER

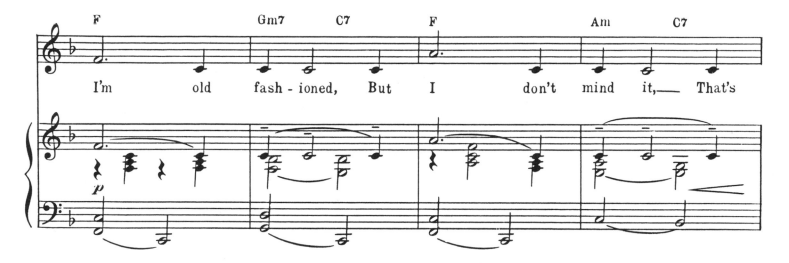

I'm old fash-ioned, But I don't mind it,___ That's

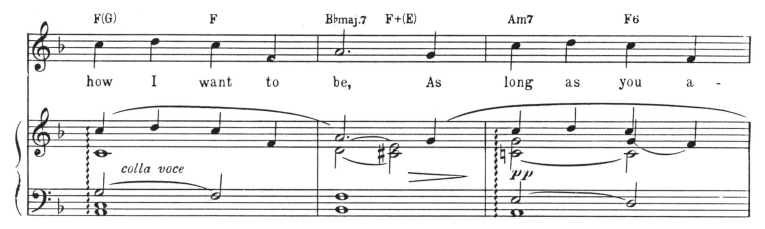

how I want to be, As long as you a-

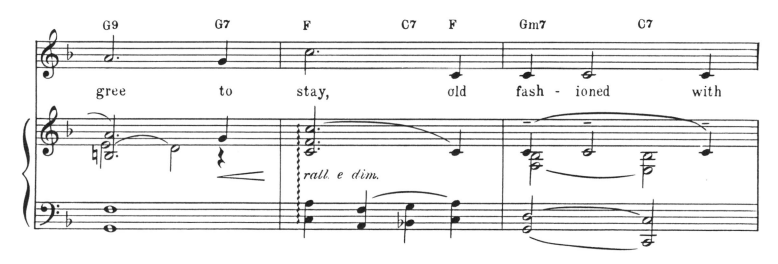

gree to stay, old fash-ioned with

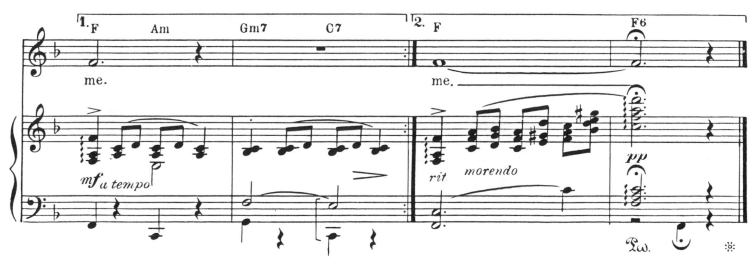

me. me.___

THE LAST TIME I SAW PARIS

from LADY BE GOOD

Lyrics by OSCAR HAMMERSTEIN II
Music by JEROME KERN

Lone - ly men with lone - ly eyes are seek-ing her in vain, Her
Chil - dren who ap - plaud- ed Punch and Ju - dy in the park, And

streets are where they were, but there's no sign of her She has left the Seine.
those who danced at night, and kept their Par - is bright Till the town went dark.

Refrain *(simply - with rhythm preserved - not sadly)*

The last time I saw Par - is Her heart was warm and

gay, I heard the laugh-ter of her heart in ev-'ry street ca-

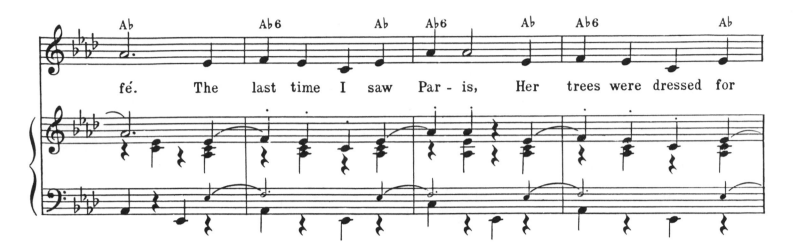

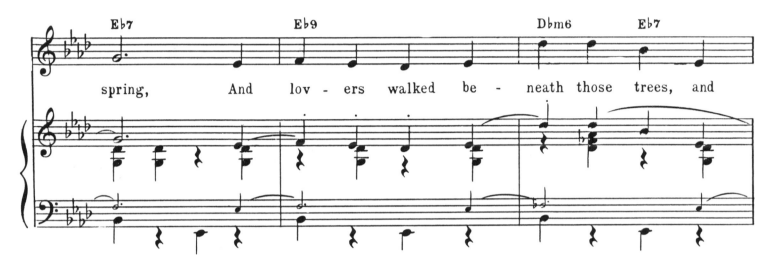

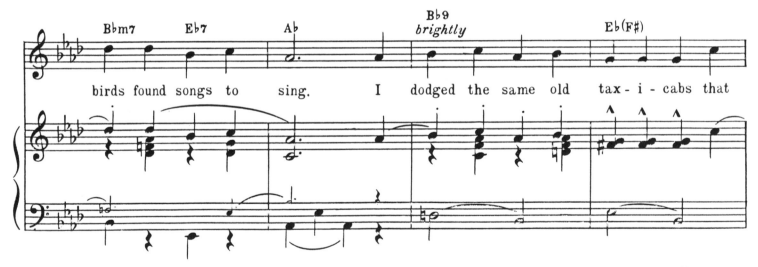

squeak-y horns was mu-sic to my ears. The last time I saw

Par-is, Her heart was warm and gay. No mat-ter how they

change her, I'll re-mem-ber her ____ that way.

2. I'll way. ____

LOOK FOR THE SILVER LINING

from SALLY

Words by BUDDY DeSYLVA
Music by JEROME KERN

Moderato

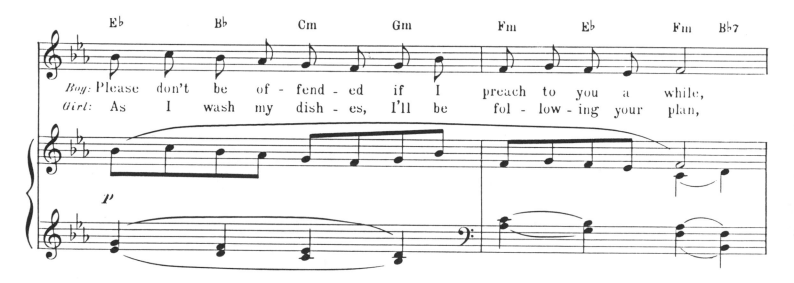

Boy: Please don't be of-fend-ed if I preach to you a while,
Girl: As I wash my dish-es, I'll be fol-low-ing your plan,

Tears are out of place in eyes that were meant to smile.
Till I see the bright-ness in ev-'ry pot and pan.

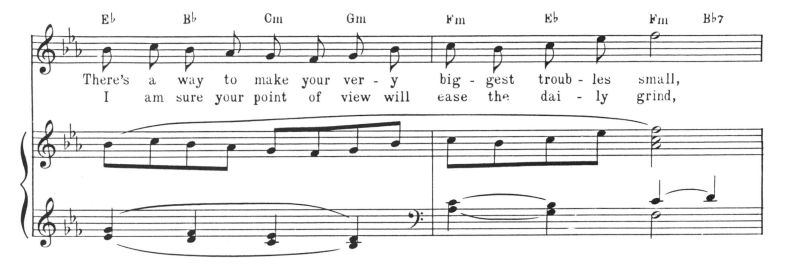

There's a way to make your ver - y big - gest troub - les small,
I am sure your point of view will ease the dai - ly grind,

Here's the hap - py se - cret of it all._____
So I'll keep re peat - ing - in my mind._____

Refrain *(slowly, with warm expression)*

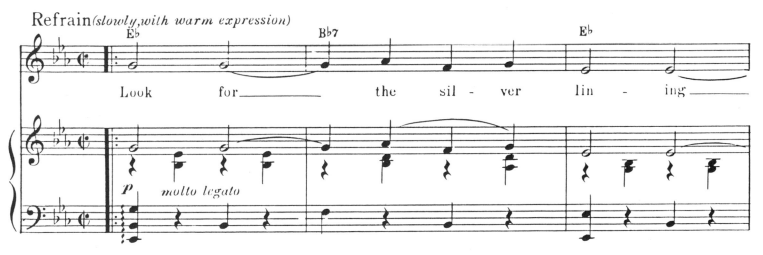

Look for_____ the sil - ver lin - ing_____

_____ When - e'er a cloud ap - pears in the

blue. _____ Re - mem - ber some where _____

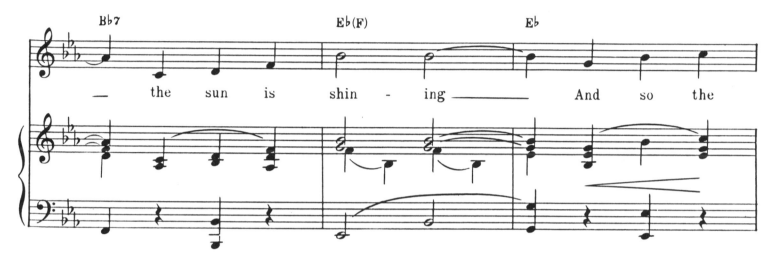

_ the sun is shin - ing _____ And so the

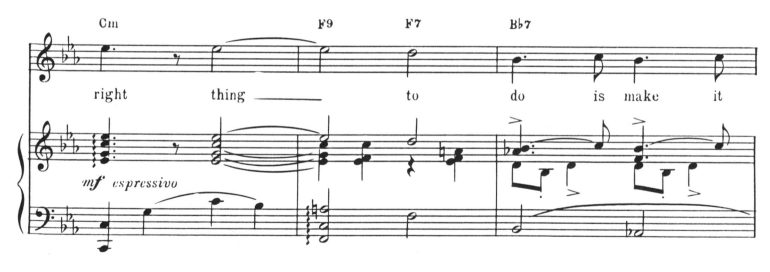

right thing _____ to do is make it

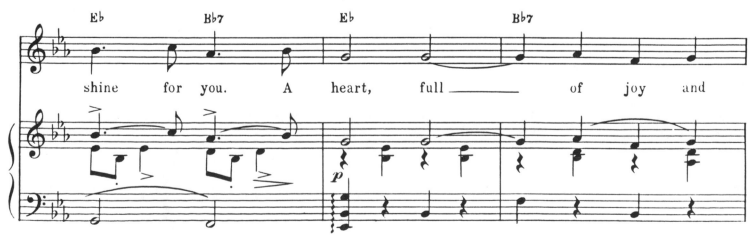

shine for you. A heart, full _____ of joy and

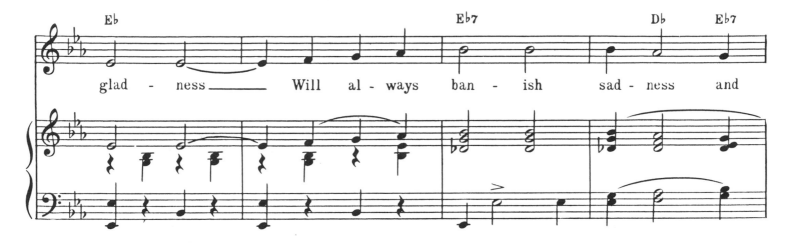

gladness_____ Will al-ways ban-ish sad-ness and

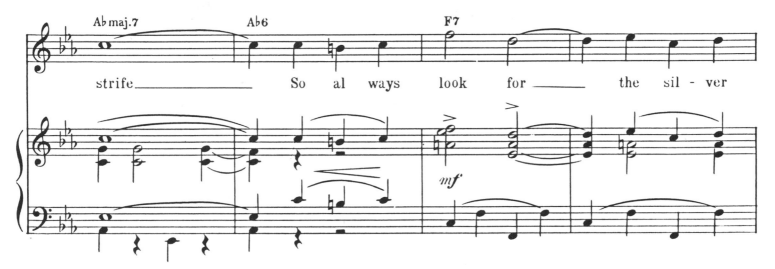

strife_____ So al-ways look for _____ the sil-ver

lin-ing _____ And try to find the sun-ny side of

life.   life._____

LOVELY TO LOOK AT
from ROBERTA

Words by DOROTHY FIELDS and JIMMY McHUGH
Music by JEROME KERN

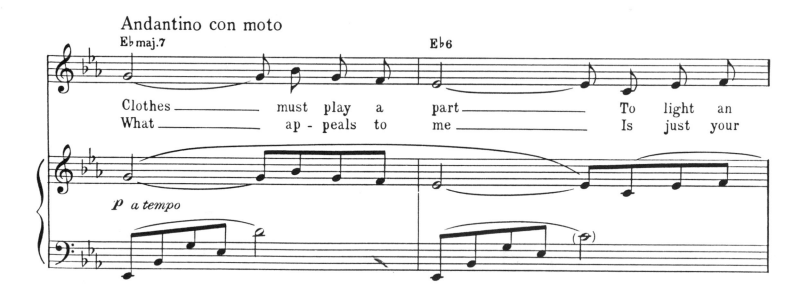

Clothes _____ must play a part _____ To light an
What _____ ap - peals to me _____ Is just your

eye, _____ to win a heart; _____ They say a
charm _____ and dig - ni - ty; _____ Not what you

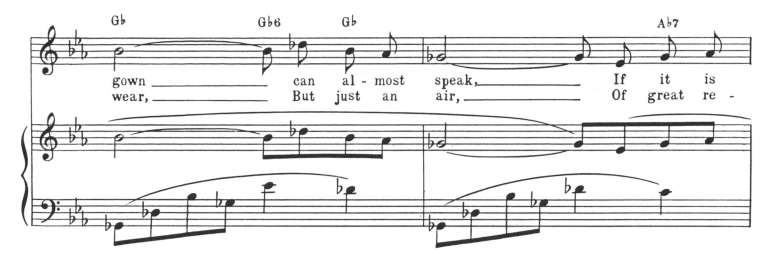

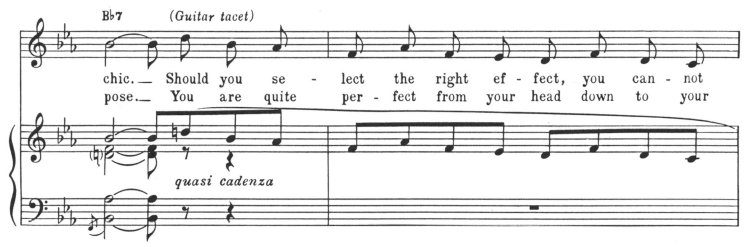

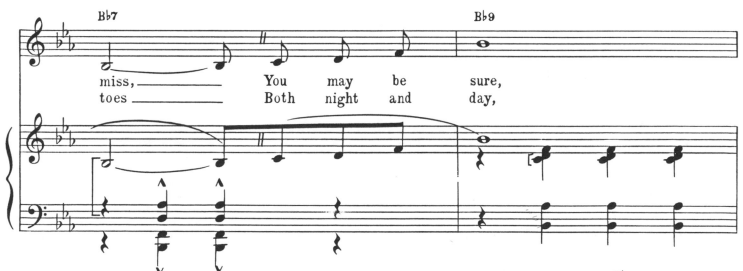

Refrain *(gracefully)*

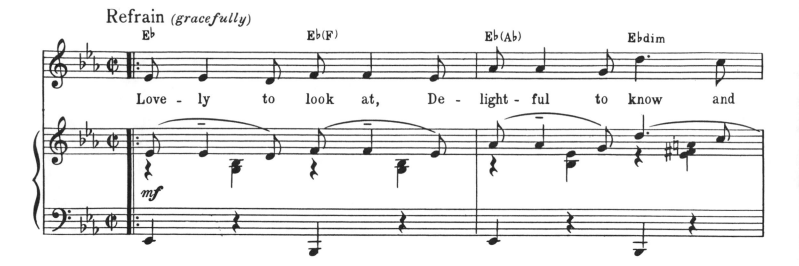

Love - ly to look at, De - light - ful to know and

heav - en to kiss. _____ A com - bin -

a - tion like this, _____ Is quite my

most im - pos - si - ble scheme come true, Im - a - gine find - ing a dream like you! You're

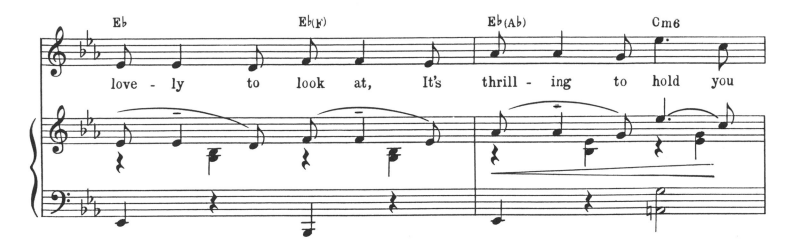

love - ly to look at, It's thrill - ing to hold you

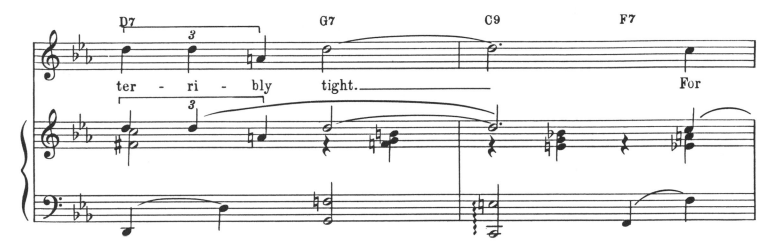

ter - ri - bly tight._____ For

we're to - geth - er, the moon is new, And oh, it's love - ly to look at you to -

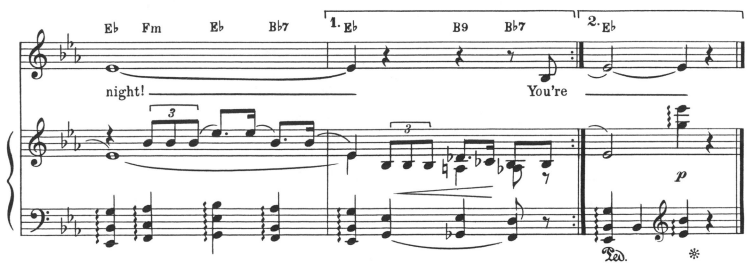

night!_____ You're _____

MAKE BELIEVE
from SHOW BOAT

Lyrics by OSCAR HAMMERSTEIN II
Music by JEROME KERN

And if the things we dream a-bout don't hap-pen_ to be so, _____

That's just an un-im-por-tant tech-ni-cal-i-ty. _____

Refrain *At a slow even pace (expressively)*

We could make be-lieve _____ I love you, _____ On-ly make be-lieve _____

_____ that you love me. _____ Oth-ers find peace of mind in pre-

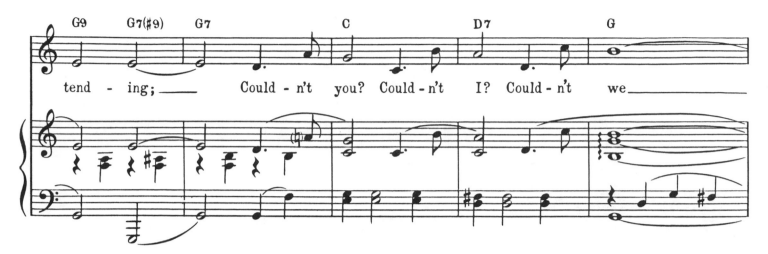

tend - ing; ____ Could - n't you? Could - n't I? Could - n't we ____

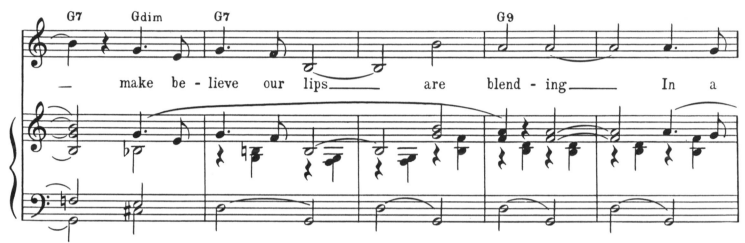

_ make be - lieve our lips ____ are blend - ing ____ In a

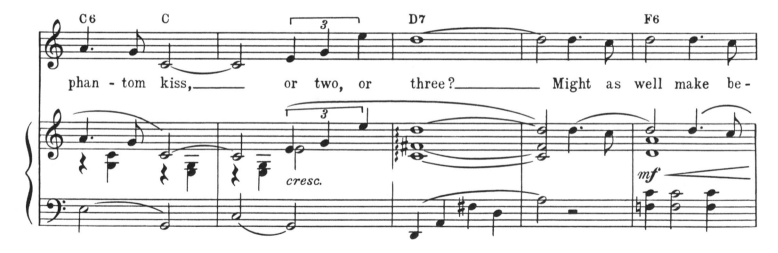

phan - tom kiss, ____ or two, or three? ____ Might as well make be -

lieve I love you, ____ For, To tell the truth, ____ I

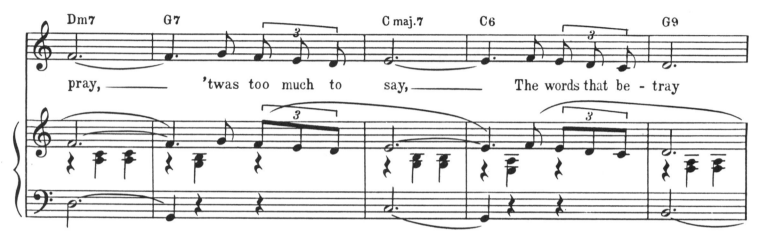

THE NIGHT WAS MADE FOR LOVE
from THE CAT AND THE FIDDLE

Words by OTTO HARBACH
Music by JEROME KERN

sweet del - i - cate charms,_____ But night time sighs for_____

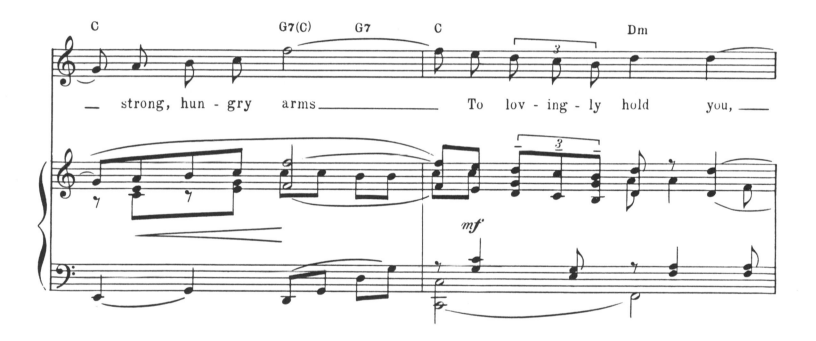

_ strong, hun - gry arms_____ To lov - ing - ly hold you,_____

_ while two lips on fire:_____ Have ar - dent - ly told you _____

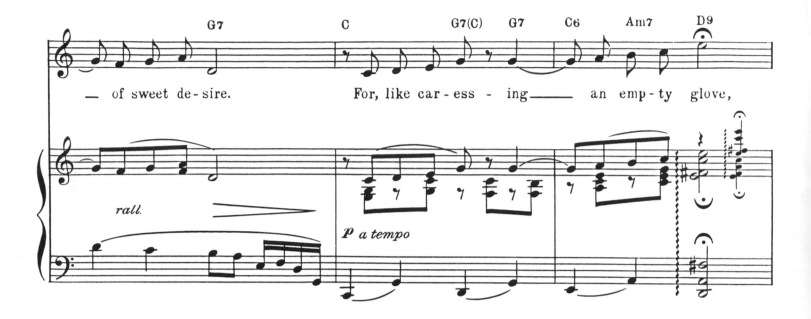

of sweet de-sire. For, like car-ess - ing_____ an emp-ty glove,

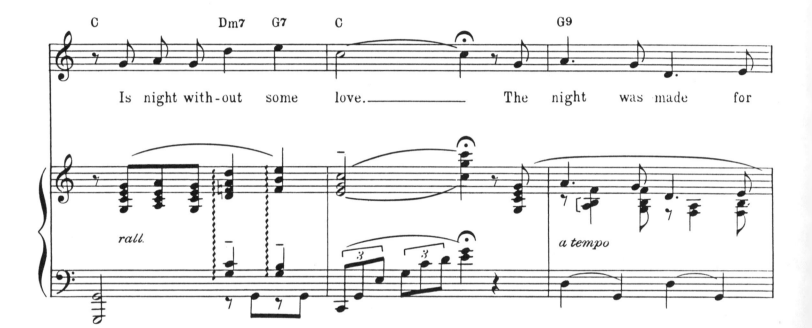

Is night with-out some love._____ The night was made for

love, The night was made for love._____

OL' MAN RIVER

from SHOW BOAT

Lyrics by OSCAR HAMMERSTEIN II
Music by JEROME KERN

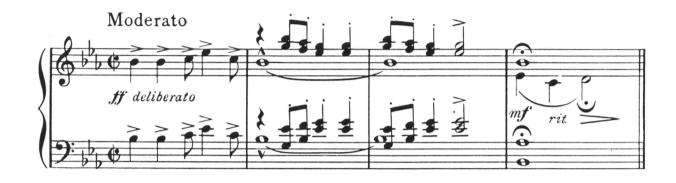

Col-ored folks work on de Mis-sis-sip-pi, Col-ored folks work while de white folks play,

Pull-in' dose boats from de dawn to sun-set, Git-tin' no rest till de judg-ment day.

66

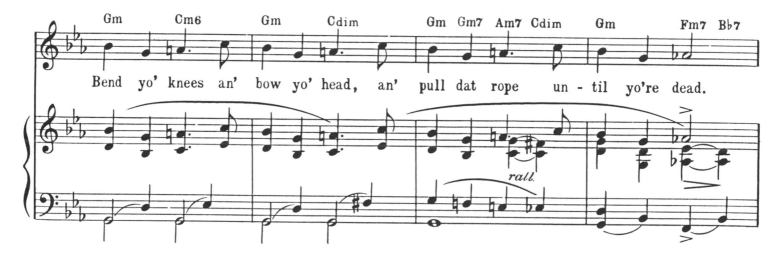

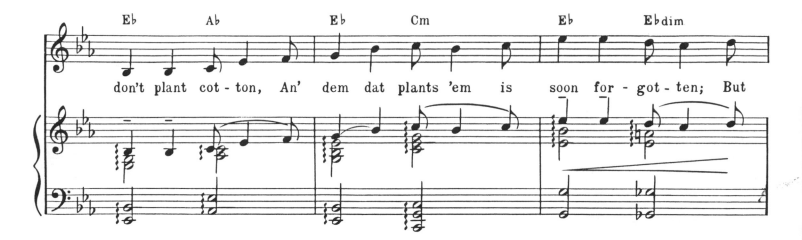

don't plant cot - ton, An' dem dat plants 'em is soon for - got - ten; But

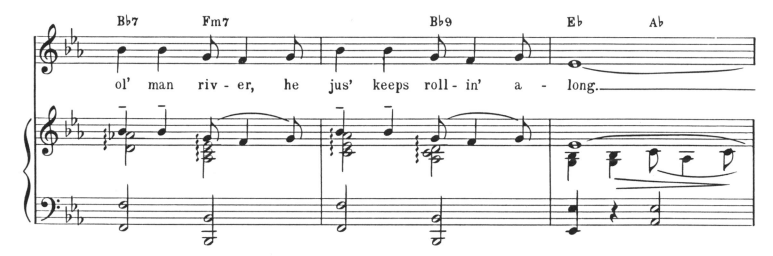

ol' man riv - er, he jus' keeps roll - in' a - long.

You an' me, we sweat an' strain,

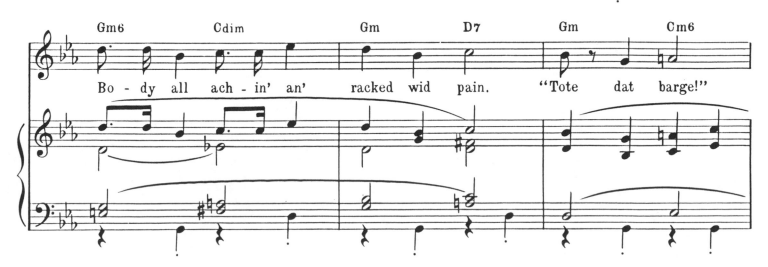

Bo - dy all ach - in' an' racked wid pain. "Tote dat barge!"

"Lift dat bale," Git a lit-tle drunk an' you land in jail.

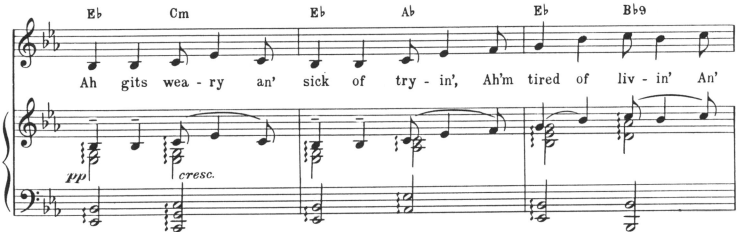

Ah gits wea-ry an' sick of try-in', Ah'm tired of liv-in' An'

skeered of dy-in', But ol' man riv-er, he jus' keeps roll-in' a-

long.

long.

PICK YOURSELF UP

from SWING TIME

Words by DOROTHY FIELDS
Music by JEROME KERN

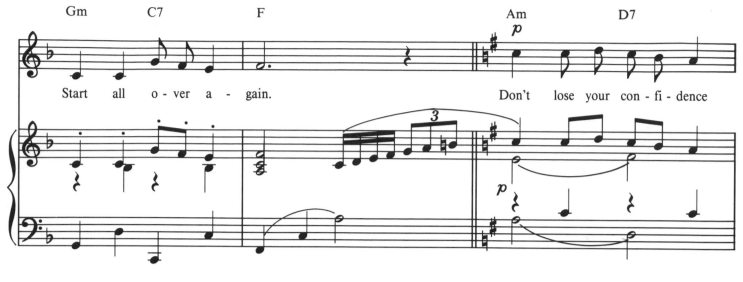

Start all o - ver a - gain.　　Don't lose your con - fi - dence

if　you　slip,　be grate - ful for　a pleas - ant　trip,　And

Pick your-self up,　Dust your-self off,　Start all o - ver a - gain.

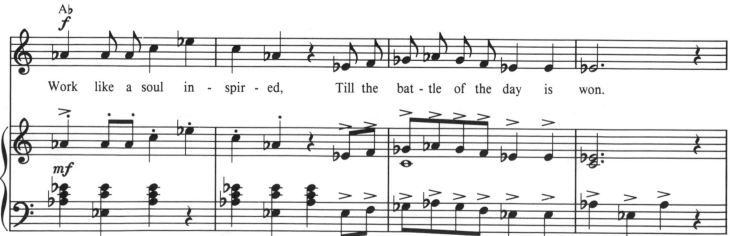

Work　like a soul in - spir - ed,　Till the bat - tle of the day is　won.

SMOKE GETS IN YOUR EYES

from ROBERTA

Words by OTTO HARBACH
Music by JEROME KERN

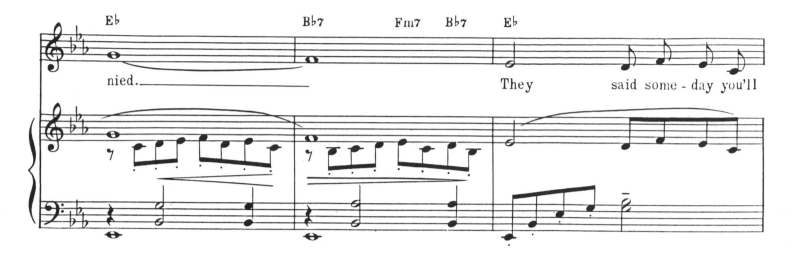

nied._____ They said some-day you'll

find, All who love are blind,_____ When your heart's on

fire, You must re-al-ize Smoke gets in your eyes._____

Un poco piu mosso

So I chaffed them and I gay-ly laughed_ to think they could doubt my

SHE DIDN'T SAY "YES"
from THE CAT AND THE FIDDLE

Words by OTTO HARBACH
Music by JEROME KERN

She did-n't say "Yes," She did-n't say "No," She did-n't say "stay," She
She did-n't say "Yes," She did-n't say "No," She want-ed to stay, But

did-n't say "go," She on-ly knew that he had spied her there____
knew she should go, She was-n't so sure that he'd be good____

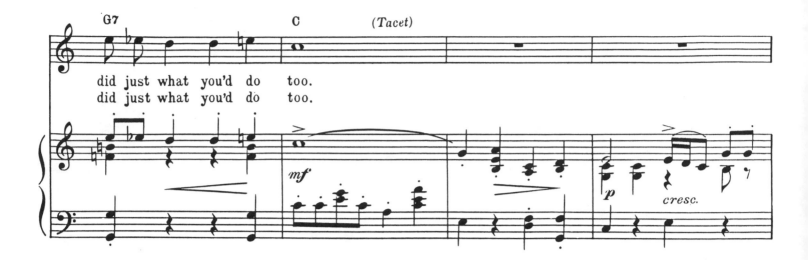

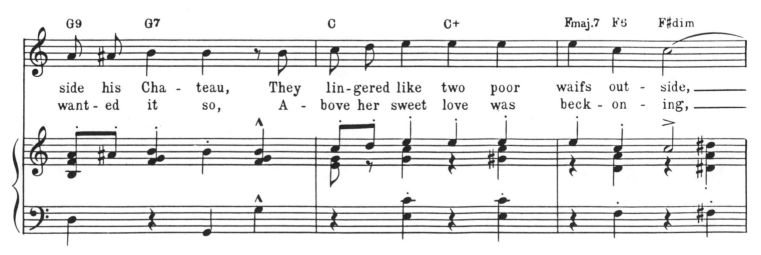

THE SONG IS YOU

from MUSIC IN THE AIR

Lyrics by OSCAR HAMMERSTEIN II
Music by JEROME KERN

let you know the song my heart would sing, _____ That beau-ti-ful

rhap-so-dy of love and youth and spring, _____ The mu-sic is

sweet, _____ The words are true, _____ The song is

you. _____

SUNNY
from SUNNY

Lyrics by OSCAR HAMMERSTEIN II and OTTO HARBACH
Music by JEROME KERN

tan - gled tress - es fly - ing o'er the hill, Heav - en bless us!

You've no less a share of Jack than Jill. You fun - ny lit - tle

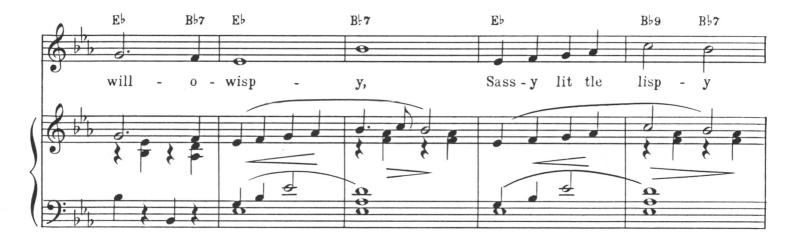

will - o - wisp - y, Sass - y lit tle lisp - y

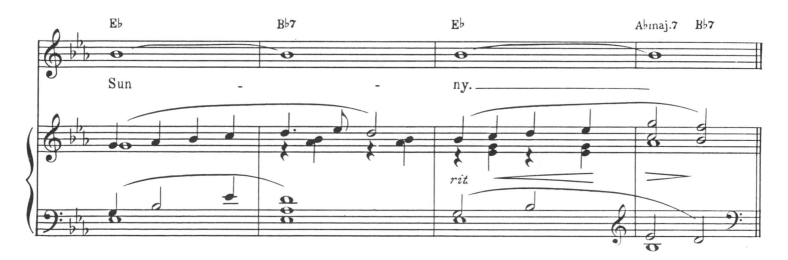

Sun - - ny.

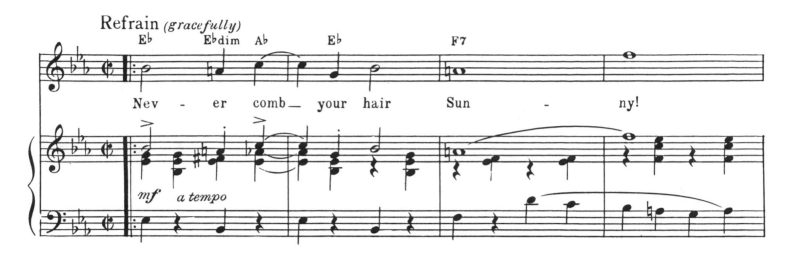

Tom ——————— boy, where'd you get —— your smile

from boy? Lit - tle sun - ny girl,

Be my hon - ey girl, I'm for

1. you! ——————— 2. you! ———————

THEY DIDN'T BELIEVE ME

from THE GIRL FROM UTAH

Words by HERBERT REYNOLDS
Music by JEROME KERN

Andante moderato

1. *He:* Got the cut-est lit-tle way, ___ Like to watch you all the
2. *She:* Don't know how it hap-pened quite, ___ May have been the sum-mer

day ___ And it cer-tain-ly seems fine ___ Just to think that you'll be
night ___ May have been, well, who can say ___ Things just hap-pen an-y

mine. ___ When I see your pret-ty smile ___
way, ___ All I know is I said "yes!" ___

Makes the liv-ing worth the while _____ So I've got to run a-
Hes-i-tat-ing more or less _____ And you kissed me where I

round _____ Tell-ing peo-ple what I've found. _____
stood _____ Just like an-y fel-low would. _____

Refrain (slowly)

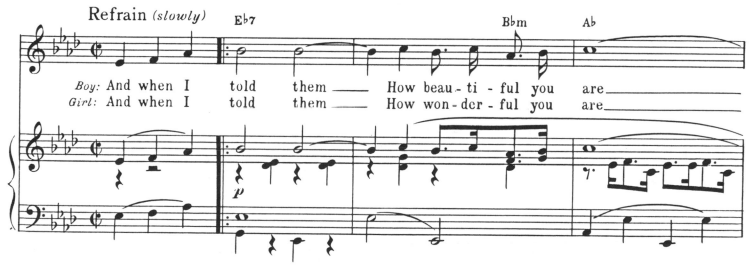

Boy: And when I told them _____ How beau-ti-ful you are _____
Girl: And when I told them _____ How won-der-ful you are _____

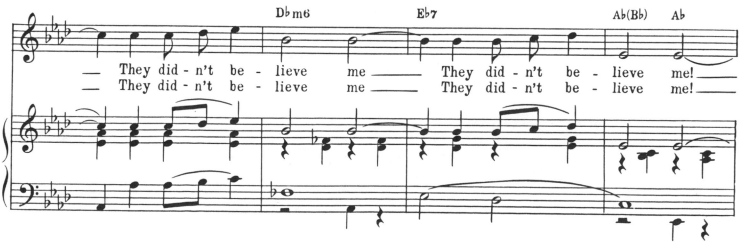

They did-n't be-lieve me _____ They did-n't be-lieve me! _____
They did-n't be-lieve me _____ They did-n't be-lieve me! _____

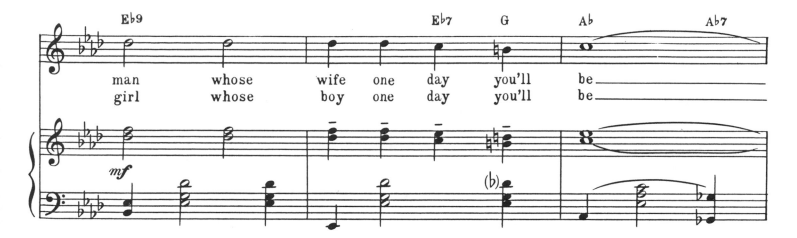

man whose wife one day you'll be_____
girl whose boy one day you'll be_____

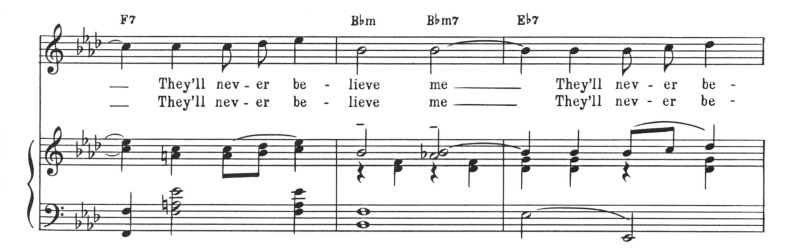

_____ They'll nev - er be - lieve me _____ They'll nev - er be -
_____ They'll nev - er be - lieve me _____ They'll nev - er be -

lieve me _____ That from this great big world you've chos - en
lieve me _____ That from this great big world you've chos - en

me! And when I me!_____

TILL THE CLOUDS ROLL BY

from OH BOY!

Words by P.G. WODEHOUSE
Music by JEROME KERN

She: I'm so sad to think that I have had to drive you from your home so
She: What bad luck, It's com-ing down in buck-ets; Have you an um-brel-la

cool-ly.   He: I'd be gain-ing noth-ing by re-main-ing,
hand-y?   He: I've a warm coat, wat-er-proof, a storm coat,

What would Mis-sus Grun-dy say? Her con-ven-tions,
I shall be all right, I know. Lat-er on, too,

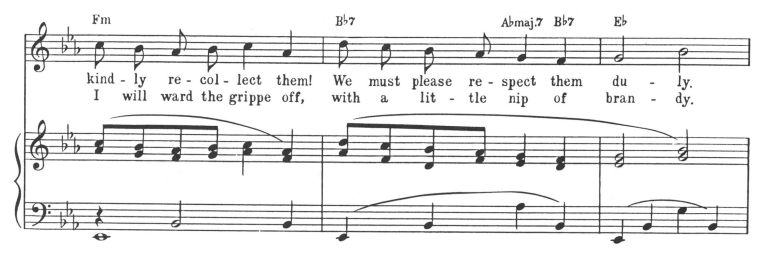

kind-ly re-col-lect them! We must please re-spect them du-ly.
I will ward the grippe off, with a lit-tle nip of bran-dy.

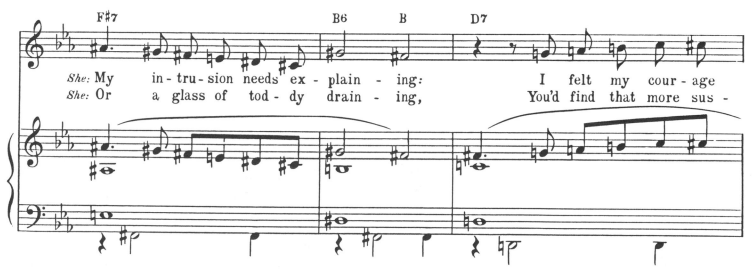

She: My in-tru-sion needs ex-plain-ing: I felt my cour-age
She: Or a glass of tod-dy drain-ing, You'd find that more sus-

wan-ing. Please, I beg don't men-tion it! I should not mind a
tain-ing. Don't be wor-ried, I en-treat, I've rub-bers for my

while the world is sleep - ing, _____ Trou - ble heap - ing

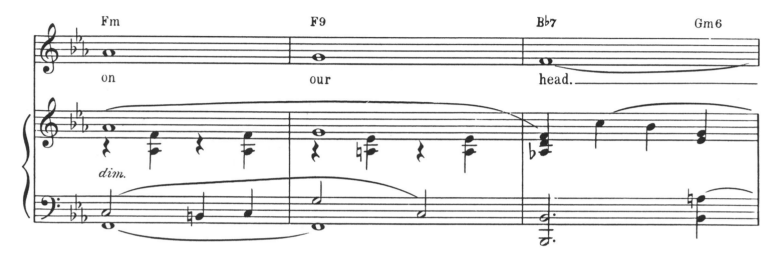

on   our   head. _____

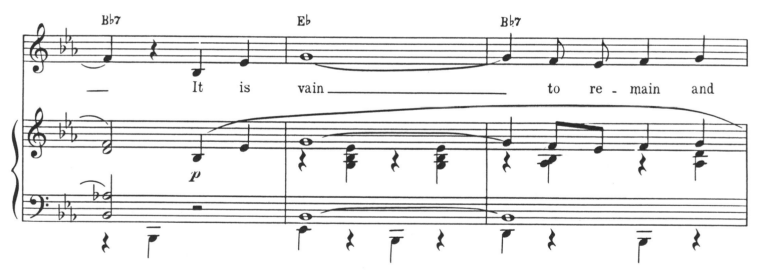

— It is vain _____ to re - main and

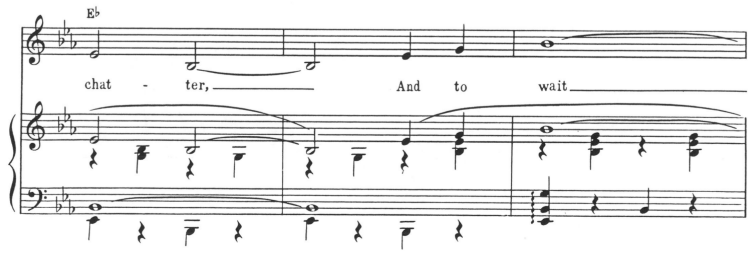

chat - ter, _____ And to wait _____

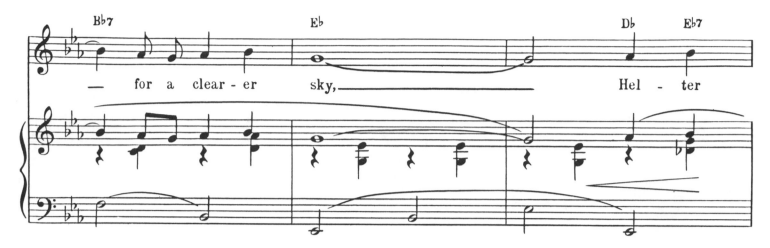

for a clear-er sky,_____ Hel - ter

skel - ter _____ I must fly for shel - ter _____

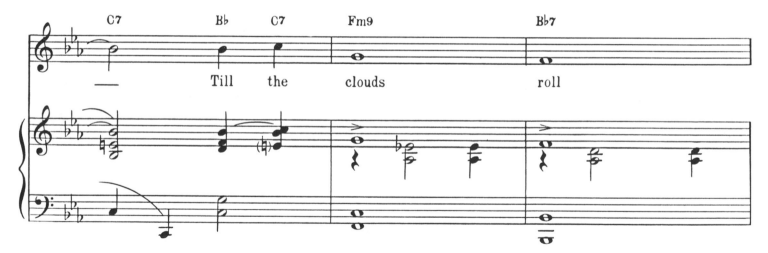

Till the clouds roll

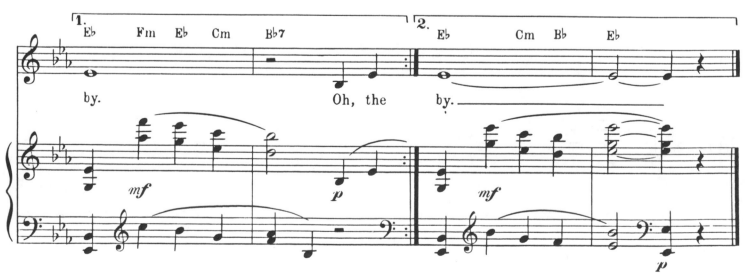

1. Oh, the
by.

2.
by. _____

WHIP-POOR-WILL
from SALLY

Words by BUD DeSYLVA
Music JEROME KERN

Mem-'ry takes me back a-way   To an ear-ly child-hood day,
While the dusk-y night bird flew   To the eve-ning ren-dez-vous,

When I stood_ with-in a lit-tle wood,_ As day was
In the dell,_ I've heard the ves-per bell,_ So soft-ly

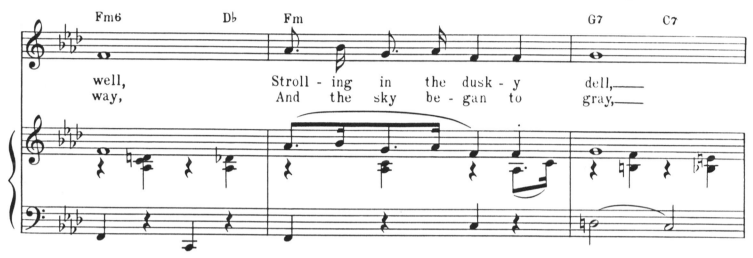

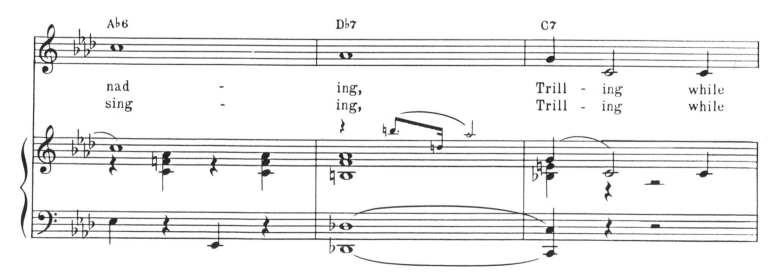

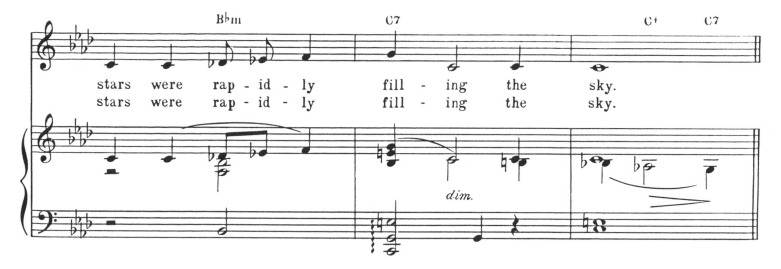

stars were rap-id-ly fill-ing the sky.
stars were rap-id-ly fill-ing the sky.

Refrain *(gracefully)*

Whip-poor-will, I used to love to hear you call to

me. Whip-poor-will,— I know he meant the world and

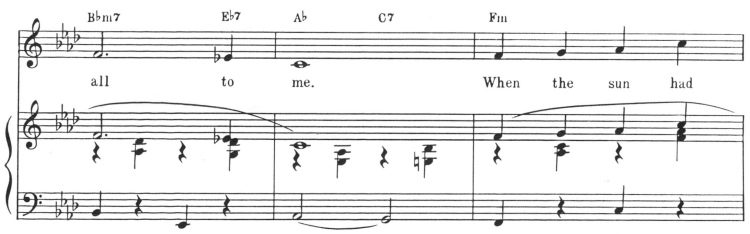

all to me. When the sun had

gone to rest,— I could hear you from your nest,— Whip-poor-will;

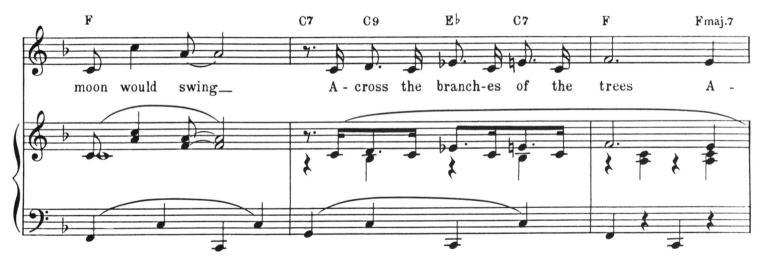

You used to whis - tle ten - der - ly._____ And when the

moon would swing— A - cross the branch-es of the trees A -

bove, You would sing— Your plain - tive lit - tle mel - o -

dies of love. Now though you're no

long - er near, In my dreams I still can hear

Whip-poor-will Ev - er call - ing to me.

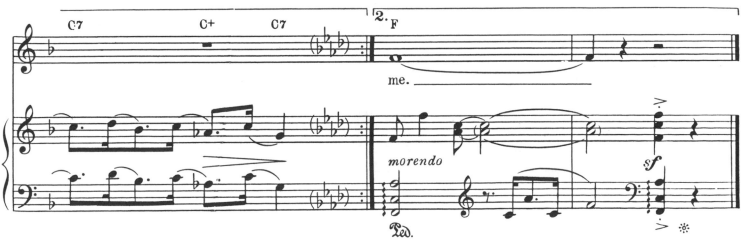

me.

THE WAY YOU LOOK TONIGHT

from SWING TIME

Words by DOROTHY FIELDS
Music by JEROME KERN

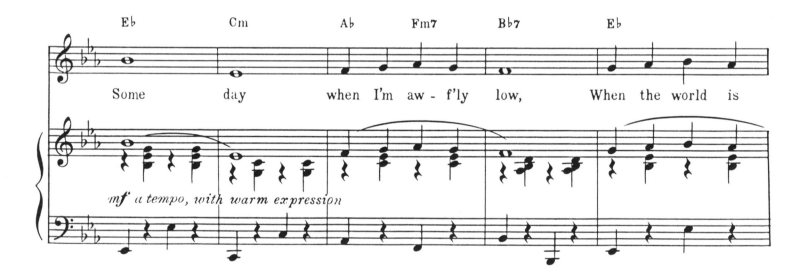

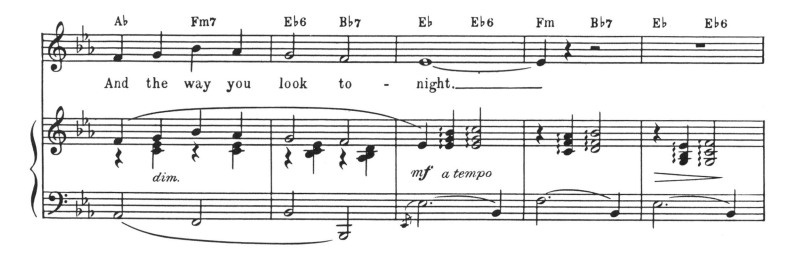

And the way you look to - night._____

Oh, but you're love - ly, With your smile so warm,

And your cheek so soft, There is noth-ing for me but to love

you, Just the way you look to - night._____

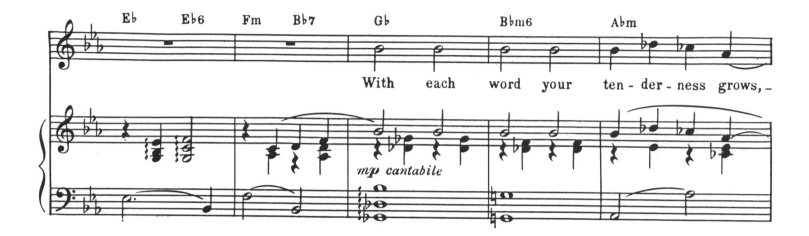

nev-er, nev-er change, Keep that breath-less charm, Won't you please ar-

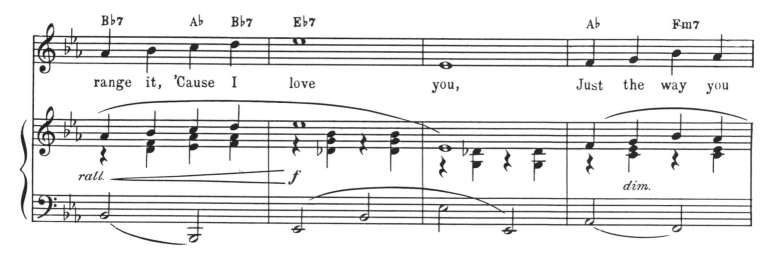

range it, 'Cause I love you, Just the way you

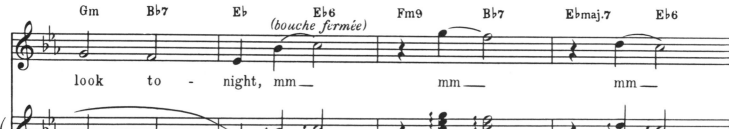

look to - night, mm— mm— mm—

mm— Just the way you look to - night.

WHO?

from SUNNY

Lyrics by OTTO HARBACH and OSCAR HAMMERSTEIN II
Music by JEROME KERN

Brightly

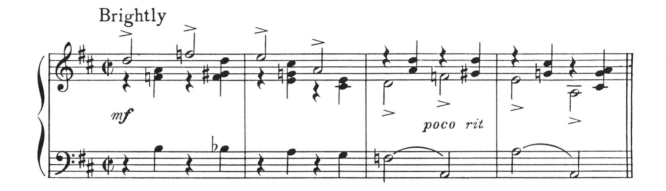

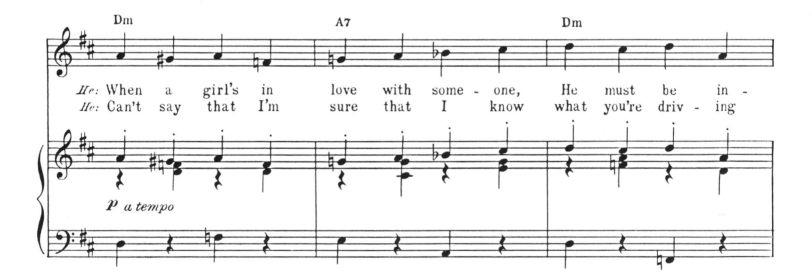

He: When a girl's in love with some-one, He must be in -
He: Can't say that I'm sure that I know what you're driv - ing

deed a dumb one If her se - cret he can - not un -
at De - ny no fur - ther if you choose to feel that

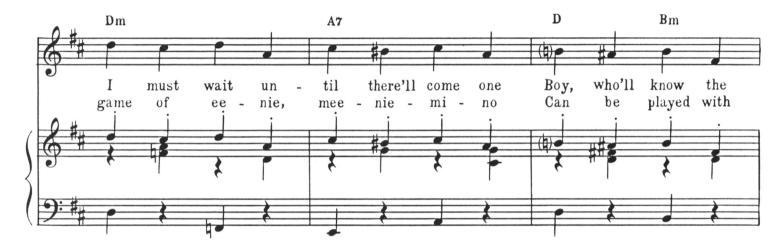

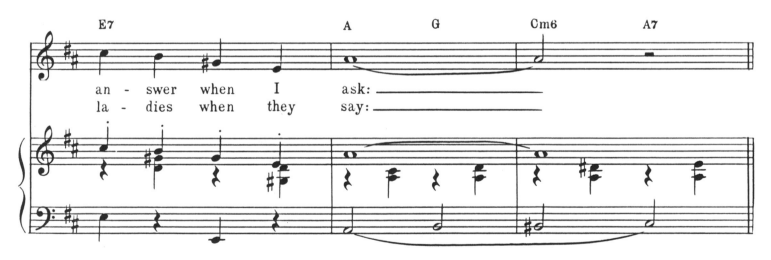

110

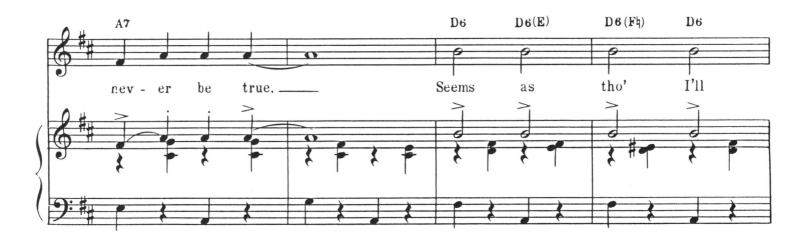

means my hap - pi - ness, Who _____

would I an - swer: "yes," to? _____

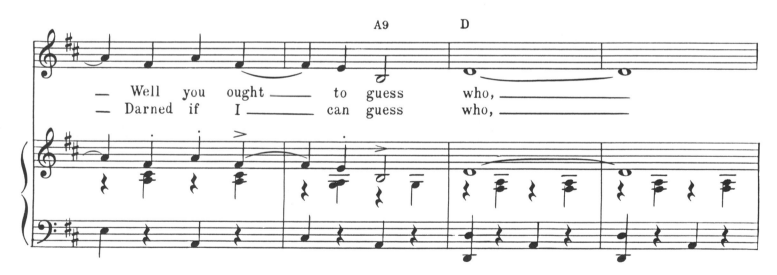

Well you ought ___ to guess who, _____
Darned if I ___ can guess who, _____

no one but you. _____

WHY DO I LOVE YOU?

from SHOW BOAT

Lyrics by OSCAR HAMMERSTEIN II
Music by JEROME KERN

I'm walk - ing on the air, dear, _____ For life is

fair, dear, _____ to lov - ers;

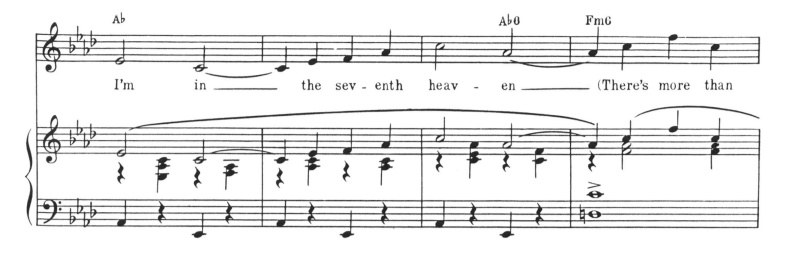

I'm in _____ the sev - enth heav - en _____ (There's more than

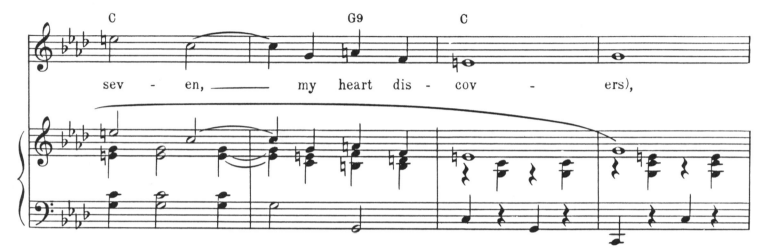

sev - en, _____ my heart dis - cov - ers),

In this sweet, im - prob - a - ble and un - real world,

Find - ing you has giv - en me my i - deal world.

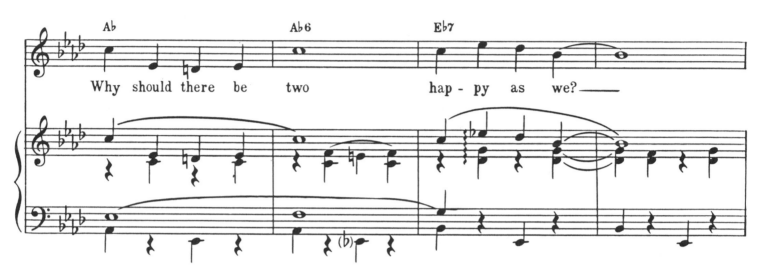

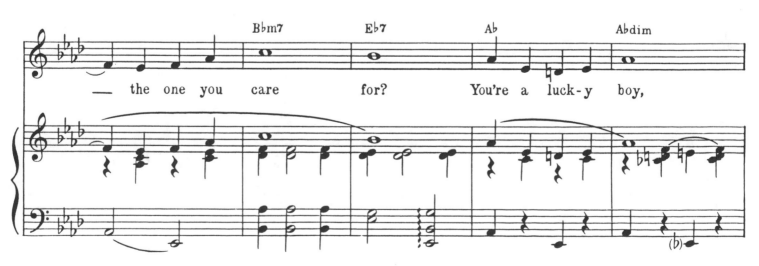

I am luck-y too, All our dreams of joy

seem to come true.____ May-be that's ____ be-cause you

love me, May-be that's why I love

you!_____ you!_____

WHY WAS I BORN?
from SWEET ADELINE

Lyrics by OSCAR HAMMERSTEIN II
Music by JEROME KERN

Andante con moto

Spend-ing these lone-some eve - nings With noth-ing to do but to live in dreams that I

make up,_____ All by my - self;_____

Dream-ing that you're be - side me, I pic - ture the pret - ti - est sto - ries on - ly to

wake up,_____ All by my - self._____

What is the good of me, by my - self?_____ _L.H._

poco rit

Refrain

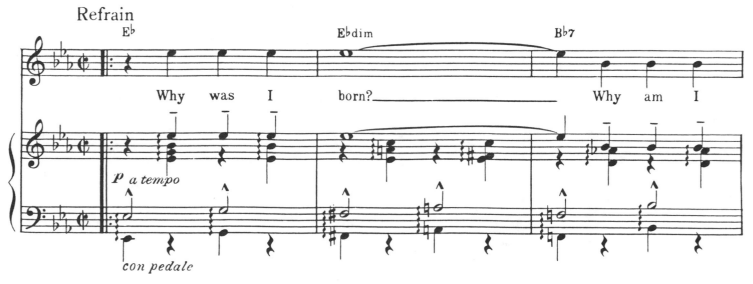

Why was I born?_____ Why am I

P a tempo

con pedale

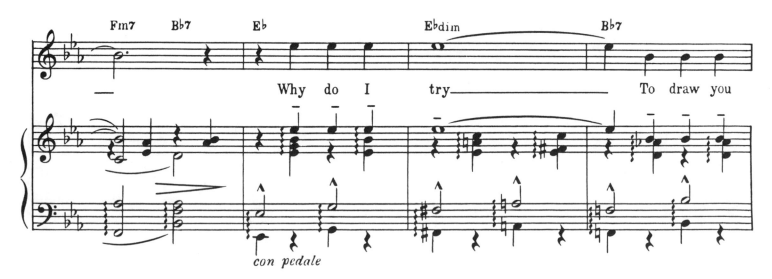

near me?_____ Why do I cry?_____ You nev - er

hear me. I'm a poor fool, but what can I

do?_____ Why was I born to love

you? you?

YOU ARE LOVE
from SHOW BOAT

Lyrics by OSCAR HAMMERSTEIN II
Music by JEROME KERN

Poco agitato

Then ___ my for - tune turned and I found ___ you;

Here ___ you are with my arms a - round ___ you.

You ___ will nev - er know what you've meant ___ to me.

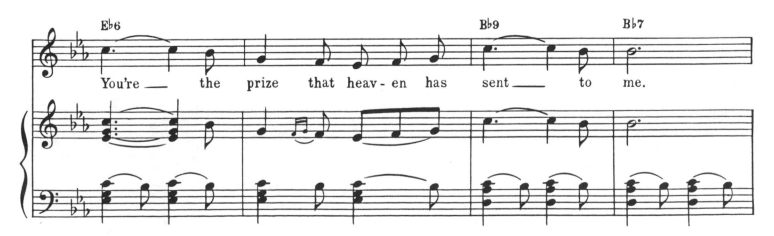

You're ___ the prize that heav - en has sent ___ to me.

Tempo di Valse

Refrain *(with expression)*

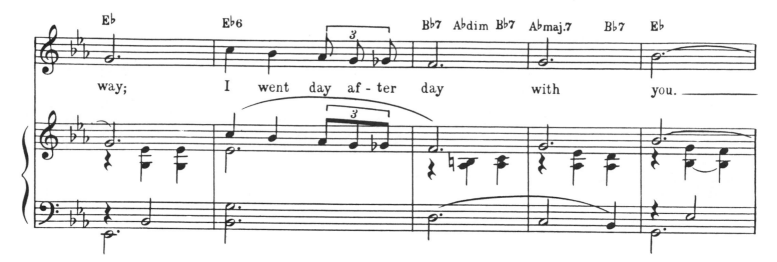

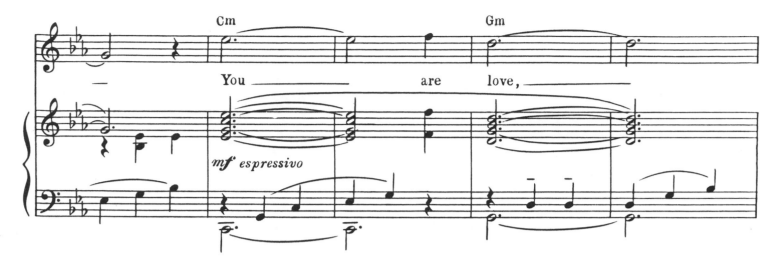

YESTERDAYS
from ROBERTA

Words by OTTO HARBACH
Music by JEROME KERN

Andantino quasi allegretto

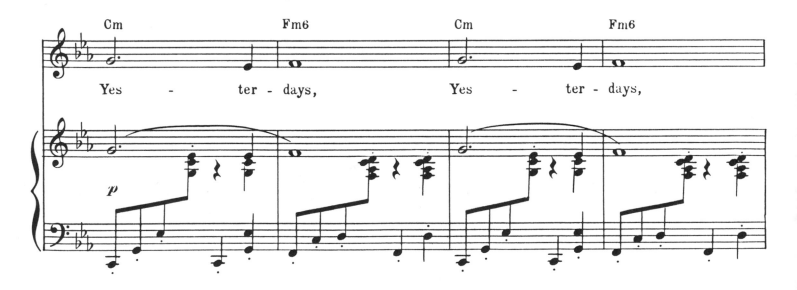

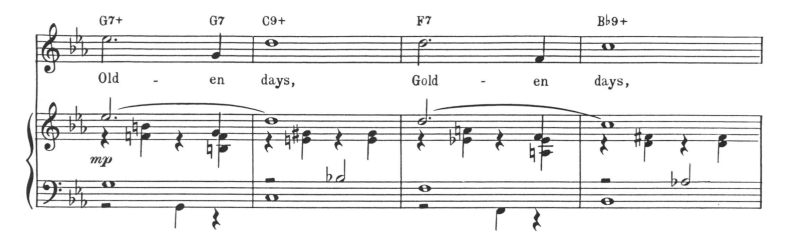

Old - en days, Gold - en days,

Days of mad ro - mance and love, Then gay

youth was mine, Truth was mine,

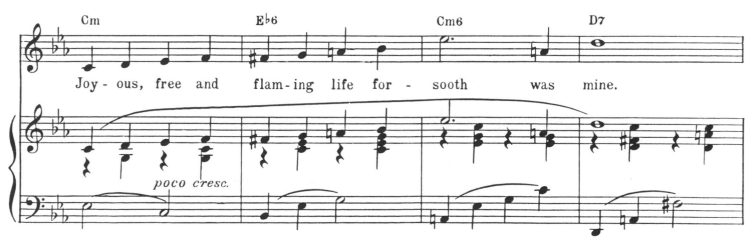

Joy - ous, free and flam - ing life for - sooth was mine.

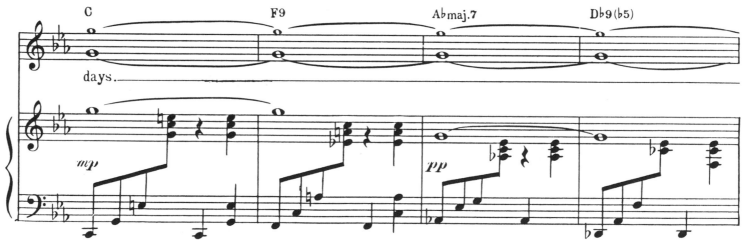

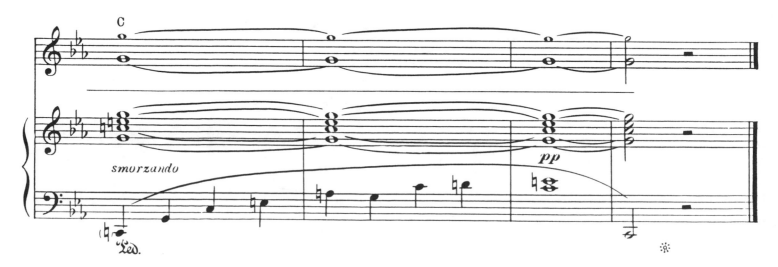